Biography of

SWAMI VIVEKANANDA

READER'S DELIGHT

AN IMPRINT OF RAMESH PUBLISHING HOUSE

NEW DELHI

ISBN: 978-93-5012-689-9
HSN Code : 49011010

Published by: Alok Kumar Gupta *for* Reader's Delight
(An Imprint of Ramesh Publishing House)

Admin. Office: 12-H, New Daryaganj Road, Opp. Officers' Mess,
New Delhi-110002 ☎ 23261567, 23275224, 23275124

Showroom: ● Balaji Market, Nai Sarak, Delhi-6 ☎ 23253720, 23282525
● 4457, Nai Sarak, Delhi-6 ☎ 23918938

E-Mail: info@rameshpublishinghouse.com
Website: www.rameshpublishinghouse.com

P*reface*

The life of Swami Vivekananda has fascinated several generations of humanity across the globe. It continues to do so even now, more than a hundred years after he departed from this world. The mission he accomplished and the tasks he performed in his very short span of existence is, indeed, bewildering. It is impossible, in the limited space we have, to take even a bird's eye view of all that he accomplished. We have therefore, touched upon his early life and the influence of his great master upon him.

There has never been a more fascinating story of a guru and disciple. The guru Sri Ramkrishna was a divinity in flesh and blood. There should not be the least doubt about that. But doubts are intrinsic to human nature. Even the great disciple Swami Vivekananda had a lingering doubt, perhaps as a brief flash of thought as to whether his master was really a divine incarnate, a Paramhamsa, or not. This doubt crept into him when the master was about to shed-off his bodily garment, when he was about to merge himself in absolute. This least doubt did not go unheeded by the master. Drawing the disciple closer, the master said, "Naren, you still have the doubts! He who was Rama in Treta Yuga and Krishna in Dwapar Yuga, is Ramakrishna in this Yuga." Even the last lingering doubt was decisively dissolved.

The inside pages contain an interesting and elevating story of how a westernized disciple, who believed in logic and reasoning and whose intellect was superlative with strong will power came gradually to believe in the Vedantic dictum of divine unity through the grace of his guru.

Publisher

Contents

INTRODUCTION

Swami Vivekananda is considered one of the most famous and influential spiritual leaders of the Vedanta philosophy and is regarded by millions of Indians as well as non-Indians as a Messenger of God.

He was the chief disciple of Ramakrishna Paramhamsa and was the founder of Ramakrishna Math and Ramakrishna Mission.

Many consider him an icon for his fearless courage, his positive exhortations to the youth, his broad outlook on social problems, and countless lectures and discourses on Vedanta philosophy.

Vivekananda is the monk who proclaimed in America, the greatness of Hinduism and of Indian culture at a time when the West regarded India as a land of barbarians.

He was the beloved disciple of Sri Ramakrishna Paramhamsa. He was the living embodiment of sacrifice and dedicated his life to the country and yearned for the progress of the poor, the helpless and the downtrodden.

He was the great thinker and mighty man of action, whose ringing words galvanized the slumbering Indians. For ages to come, he will be a source of inspiration.

THE MISCHIEVOUS BOY

Swami Vivekananda came to be known by this name, only when he became a sannyasi or monk. His parents called him Narendra. His father was Vishwanatha Datta and his mother Bhuvaneshwari Devi. Narendra was born on 12, January 1863, in Calcutta (now Kolkata). As a child, he was very lively and naughty.

Even as he was young, he showed a precocious mind and keen memory. He practiced meditation from a very early age. While in school, he was good at studies, as well as sports and the other activities of various kinds. He organised an amateur theatrical company and a gymnasium and took lessons in fencing, wrestling, rowing and other sports. He also studied instrumental and vocal music. He was a leader among his group of friends. Even when he was young, he questioned the validity of superstitious customs and discrimination based on caste and religion.

When Narendra stepped into boyhood, his naughtiness grew. He was a natural leader of the children in the neighbourhood. His companions always bowed to his decision. Narendra loved to tease his sisters.

Once a landlord threatened the children saying, "There is a demon in the tree and he swallows children." Narendra was not impressed by this threat. He settled down on a branch. The other boys took to their heels. Narendra waited for several hours, but the demon did not appear. So, he declared that the landlord's story was funny. Meditation, too, was a sport to him. But as he meditated, he became oblivious of the whole world. Not even a lizard or a snake moving near him could disturb his concentration.

Even as a child Narendra had great respect for sannyasis or ascetics. He would give away anything to anybody, if asked for. On his birthday, he would wear new clothes. If a beggar asked for alms, he would give away the new clothes. For that day, his mother would lock him up in a room whenever a beggar passed by the house. But every beggar knew Narendra's nature very well. They would stand near the window of his room. He would throw to them anything he had. The spirit of sacrifice and renunciation was already blossoming in him.

In his leisure time, his mother would tell him the story of the Ramayana. He could not sleep unless she told him a story. Then, he would be all ears, forgetting his study and play. He had great reverence for Lord Hanuman. Once, he sat before the idol of Lord Shiva, with his body all smeared with ash. His perplexed mother asked him, "Naren, what's all this?" He smiled and said, "Mother, I'm Lord Shiva." The mother feared that her son would become a sannyasi, like his grandfather.

Narendra's father was a lawyer. So, every day his house used to be crowded with his clients belonging to different castes. The house was like an inn; the clients had breakfast and lunch there. It was the custom to provide the guests with *hukkas* (long pipes) to smoke after food. There was a different pipe for clients of each caste. Narendra wondered what would happen, if he smoked the pipe meant for people of a different caste. Finally he experimented and nothing untoward happened. He concluded that caste had no meaning.

The maxim 'The child is father of the man' was entirely true of the compassionate boy, Narendra. Once, there was a display of physical exercises in a local gymnasium. Accidentally, an iron bar fell on a sailor among the spectators. He fell down unconscious. The people, who had gathered there ran away, lest the police should question them. Narendra, with the help of two friends of his, gave the wounded sailor first aid. Then he took him to a doctor. He even raised some money for the wounded man. On another occasion, Narendra pulled out one of his friends, who had been caught under the wheel of a coach drawn by horses. Likewise, he helped a little boy who was a total stranger. The boy was lying on a road with high fever. He took him home. Narendra never knew, what fear was.

It was not that Narendra excelled only in sports; he was quick and alert in his studies as well. After a single reading, he could remember any lesson. His memory was amazing. Concentration was the key to his success in studies.

In 1879, Narendra entered the Presidency College, Calcutta for higher studies. After one year, he joined the Scottish Church College, Calcutta and studied philosophy. During the course, he studied western logic, western philosophy and history of European nations.

Questions started to arise in young Narendra's mind about God and the presence of God. This made him associate with the *Brahmo Samaj,* an important religious movement of the time, led by Keshab Chandra Sen. But the Samaj's congregational prayers and devotional songs could not satisfy Narendra's zeal to realise God. He would ask leaders of *Brahmo Samaj,* whether they had seen God. He never got a satisfying answer. It was during this time that Professor Hastie of Scottish Church College told him about Sri Ramakrishna of Dakshineswar.

THE PARENTS

Whenever Vishwanath Datta found time, he would give his son advice, "You need fear no one so long as you keep to the path of truth and Dharma. One should not be browbeaten. One should guard one's self-respect. Love of one's religion should not mean hatred of others' religions. Patriotism is essential for man's welfare. Foreign enemies may invade a country, but they cannot take away people's ancient and potent culture." He loved to listen to his son's sweet voice. Narendra's face would become radiant when he sang devotional songs.

His mother was dear to Narendra as his own life, and to him, she was a veritable goddess. In his eyes, there was no one as ready to make sacrifices as the mother. She must have the highest place not only in the home but also in society. He had great respect for his father too. But this did not come in the way of his freedom and independent thinking.

He gave expression to what he felt even about his father. "Hospitality is certainly a great virtue. But is it right to feed the lazy? Is it right to provide them with cigarette and pipe to smoke?" This, he would often question his father. But his father would say, "You do not understand their misery, my boy. When they take much tobacco, they at least, for a while forget the bitterness of their life."

By 1880, Narendra passed his Matriculation and Entrance Examination. He joined a college. Day by day, his thirst for knowledge increased. He would borrow from the library, books not related to the prescribed courses and read them, and so satisfy his thirst. He was particularly fascinated by the secrets of God's creation. Apart from history and science, he was well read in Western philosophy. As he advanced in his studies, his thinking faculty developed. Doubts and uncertainties overtook him. He gave up blind beliefs, but could not realize the Truth.

He placed his doubts before eminent scholars and sought their guidance. These scholars excelled in debate. But their logic did not convince Narendra. Their line of thinking was stale. It did not convince him, for none of them had direct experience of God.

— *** —

SEARCHING THE GURU

Sri Ramakrishna was a priest in the temple of Goddess Kali. He was not a scholar. But he was a great devotee. It was being said of him that he had realized God. Scholars who went to him became his disciples.

In 1884, when Narendranath was preparing for the B.A. examination, his family was struck by a calamity. His father suddenly died, and the mother and children were plunged into great grief. For Viswanath, a man of generous nature, had lived beyond his means, and his death burdened the family with a heavy debt. Creditors, like hungry wolves, began to prowl about the door, and to make matters worse, certain relatives brought a lawsuit for the partition of the ancestral home. Though they lost it, Narendra was faced, thereafter, with poverty. As the eldest male member of the family, he had to find a means for the feeding of seven or eight mouths and began to hunt a job. He also attended the law classes.

He went about clad in coarse clothes, barefeet, and hungry. Often, he refused invitations for dinner from friends, remembering his starving mother, brothers, and sisters at home.

The Datta family was proud and would not dream of soliciting help from outsiders. His rich friends no doubt noticed his pale face, but they did nothing to help him. Only one friend sent occasional anonymous aid, and Narendra remained grateful to him for life.

Meanwhile, all his efforts to find employment failed. Some friends, who earned money in a dishonest way asked him to join them, and a rich woman sent him an immoral proposal, promising to put an end to his financial distress. But Narendra gave to these a blunt rebuff. Sometimes, he would wonder if the world were not the handiwork of the Devil— for how could one account for so much suffering in God's creation?

One day, after a futile search for a job, he sat down, weary and footsore, in the big park of Calcutta in the shadow of the Ochterlony monument. There some friends joined him and one of them sang a song, perhaps to console him, describing God's abundant grace.

Bitterly Naren said: "Will you please stop that song? Such fancies are, no doubt, pleasing to those who are born with silver spoons in their mouths. Yes, there was a time when I, too, thought like that. But today, these ideas appear to me a mockery." The friends were bewildered.

One morning, as usual, Naren left his bed repeating God's name, and was about to go out in search of work after seeking the divine blessings. His mother heard the prayer and said bitterly: 'Hush, you fool! You have been crying yourself hoarse for God since your childhood. Tell me, what has God done for you?' Evidently, the crushing poverty at home was too much for the pious mother. These words stung Naren to the quick. A doubt crept into his mind about God's existence and His Providence.

It was not in Naren's nature to hide his feelings. He argued before his friends and the devotees of Sri Ramakrishna about God's non-existence and the futility of prayer even if God existed. His over-zealous friends thought he had become an atheist and ascribed to him many unmentionable crimes, which he had supposedly committed to forget his misery. Some of the devotees of the Master shared these views.

Narendra was angry and mortified to think that they could believe him to have sunk so low. He became hardened and justified drinking and the other dubious pleasures resorted to by miserable people for a respite from their suffering. He said, further, that he himself would not hesitate to follow such a course, if he were assured of its efficacy. Openly asserting that only cowards believed in God for fear of hell-fire, he argued the possibility of God's non-existence and quoted Western philosophers in support of his position. And when the devotees of the Master became convinced that he was hopelessly lost, he felt a sort of inner satisfaction.

A garbled report of the matter reached Sri Ramakrishna, and Narendra thought that perhaps the Master, too, doubted his moral integrity. The very idea revived his anger. "Never mind," he said to himself, "If good or bad opinion of a man rests on such flimsy grounds, I don't care."

But Narendra was mistaken. For one day Bhavanath, a devotee of the master and an intimate friend of Narendra, cast aspersions on the latter's character, and the Master said angrily: "Stop, you fool! The Mother has told me that it is simply not true. I shan't look at your face, if you speak to me again that way."

The fact was that Narendra could not, in his heart of hearts, disbelieve in God. He remembered the spiritual visions of his own boyhood and many others that he had experienced in the company of the Master. Inwardly, he longed to understand God and his ways.

One day, he had been out since morning in a soaking rain in search of employment, having had neither food nor rest for the whole day. That evening he sat down on the porch of a house by the roadside, exhausted. He was in a daze. Thoughts began to open before his mind, which he could not control. Suddenly he had a strange vision, which lasted almost the whole night. He felt that veil after veil opened up, out of his soul, and God's justice with mercy was clear to him.

He came to know, but he never told how that misery could exist in the creation of a compassionate God without impairing his sovereign power or touching man's real self. He understood the meaning of it all and was at peace. Just before daybreak, refreshed both in body and in mind, he returned home.

This revelation profoundly impressed Narendranath. He became indifferent to people's opinion and was convinced that he was not born to lead an ordinary worldly life, enjoying the love of a wife and children and physical luxuries. He determined to renounce the world, and set a date for this act. Then, coming to learn that Sri Ramakrishna would visit Calcutta that very day, he was happy to think that he could embrace the life of a wandering monk with his guru's blessings.

When they met, the Master persuaded his disciple to accompany him to Dakshineswar. As they arrived in his room, Sri Ramakrishna went into an ecstatic mood and sang a song, while tears bathed his eyes. The words of the song clearly indicated that the Master knew of the disciple's secret wish.

When other devotees asked him about the cause of his grief, Sri Ramakrishna said, *"Oh, never mind, it is something between me and Naren, and nobody else's business."* At night he called Naren to his side and said with great feeling: "I know you are born for Mother's work. I also know that you will be a monk. But stay in the world as long as I live, for my sake at least."

Soon after, Naren procured a temporary job, which was sufficient to provide a hand-to-mouth living for the family. Sri Ramakrishna's behaviour puzzled Narendra. He thought the elderly man was mad. "Will you come again? Promise me you will", pleaded Ramakrishna. Eager to escape from him, Narendra said, "Yes".

After the Bhagavan finished his discourse, Narendra asked him, "Have you seen God?" "Of course I have. I see him just as I see you, only more clearly. I have even talked to him. I can show him to you. But who is yearning to see God?" replied Ramakrishna. Narendra said to himself, "Till today no one had told me he had seen God. This man looks mentally deranged; possibly, he is even mad. However, it is not proper to judge without investigating."

A month passed. Narendra went alone to Dakshineswar. Ramakrishna was resting on a cot in his room. He was pleased to see Narendra; he asked him to sit on his cot. He went into a trance and put his leg on Narendra's lap. Narendra forgot the outer world. He felt that he was dissolving. He shouted, "What's this you are doing to me? My parents are still alive. I should go back to them." Smilingly Sri Ramakrishna said, "Enough for today," and drew back his leg. Narendra became normal once again.

— ✳✳✳ —

THE TEST

As days passed, each was attracted towards the other. Neither could bear to be parted from the other. It did not take long for Sri Ramakrishna to realize the greatness of Narendra. Moreover, he was guided by the will of Goddess Kali.

But young Narendra would not accept Ramakrishna as his guru without a test.

Ramakrishna used to say that in order to realize God, one should give up the desire for money and women. One day Narendra hid a rupee under his pillow. Sri Rama krishna, who had gone out, came into the room and stretched himself on the cot. At once he jumped up as if bitten by a scorpion. When he shook the mattress, the rupee coin fell down. Later, he came to know that it was the doing of Narendra.

Narendra was Ramakrishna's favourite disciple. But he would not accept as gospel truth all that his guru said. Narendra was highly critical of people, who worshipped idols. He rejected the theory of "Advaita" (monism). He had no faith in mystic experiences. Advaitic assertions such as "I am Brahman", "I am

Shiva" did not impress Narendra. But Sri Ramakrishna would always bring him back to the right path by saying, "There are many roads to reach a destination. No one has the right to say that the path the other man takes is not the right one. It is improper to pass judgement on anything that one does not understand."

One day Sri Ramakrishna took Narendra to a secluded place. He said, "I have attained some powers after a long period of meditation. They will give whatever a man wants. I have given up all desires, and so I have no use for these powers. Shall I bestow these powers on you?" "But will they help me to realize the Self?" asked Narendra. "No," said Sri Ramakrishna. "Then I do not want them. More than anything, I want to realize God." Narendra's reply filled Ramakrishna with joy. The Master had tested Narendra, and Narendra had passed the test.

Gradually, Narendra turned towards renunciation, giving up all worldly desires. The parents came to know of this. He was then studying for his BA degree examination. They planned to bring him back to worldly life through marriage. Sri Ramakrishna became unhappy on hearing this. He advised Narendra that if he bound himself by family ties, he would not be able to serve mankind. At times, Narendra would lose faith in Ramakrishna, but the guru would touch him with his hands. Then Narendra would lose contact with the world around. After regaining his consciousness, he would surrender to his Guru's teaching. Thus, the Guru gradually gifted all his powers to the disciple.

In 1884, Narendra passed the BA degree examination. A friend of his hosted a party. As Narendra was singing at the party, the news of his father's death came like a bolt from the blue.

One day he said to himself: "God gives whatever my Guru seeks. So it is best to seek my Guru's help." He went straight to his Guru and said, "On my behalf, kindly pray before the Goddess to rid me of this poverty. She will give you whatever you wish for, won't She?" The Guru said, "My child, you have no faith in Her, why then will She listen to my prayer? You approach Her yourself. Then she will fulfill your need." So in the dead of the night, Narendra stood before the idol of Goddess Kali. He lost himself in deep meditation. He begged the Goddess, "O Mother, bestow on me the spirit of renunciation. Let me see you, that is all I beg of you."

When he came out, the Guru asked, "Did you submit your prayer to Her? And what did She say?" Narendra said in dismay, "O! Forgot about it completely." "Then go back and ask Her," said the Guru. Again he forgot to speak about his poverty in his prayer to the Goddess.

Again the Guru sent him. Back came Narendra and the same thing happened. The Guru's joy knew no bounds. "My child, you should not crave for only food and clothes. They are not the ultimate goals of man.

Have faith in God. He will look after the welfare of your family," said the Guru.

Later, Narendra took up the profession of teaching. For some time, he taught in the Vidyasagar School. Now the family had at least enough food. While he worked as a teacher, he continued his study of law. His Guru's health broke down. Sri Ramakrishna developed a tumour in the throat. Narendra gave up both, his job and his studies, and devoted all his time to nursing his Master.

Once, while Narendra was in meditation he shouted, "Where is my body?" Others had to touch his body and convince him of its existence. When Sri Ramakrishna heard this episode, he was happy that at last his desire to find a worthy disciple had been fulfilled.

In time, Narendra accepted Ramakrishna, and while he accepted, his acceptance was whole-hearted. While Ramakrishna predominantly taught duality and Bhakti to his other disciples, he taught Narendra the Advaita Vedanta, the philosophy of non-dualism.

During the course of five years of his training under Ramakrishna, Narendra was transformed from a restless, puzzled, impatient youth to a mature man who was ready to renounce everything for the sake of God-realisation.

— *** —

FUN WITH THE MASTER

It is hard to say when Naren actually accepted Sri Ramakrishna as his guru. As far as the master was concerned, the spiritual relationship was established at the first meeting at Dakshineswar, when he had touched Naren, stirring him to his inner depths. From that moment, he had an implicit faith in the disciple and bore him a great love. But he encouraged Naren in the independence of his thinking. The love and faith of the Master acted as a restraint upon the impetuous youth and became his strong shield against the temptations of the world. By gradual steps, the disciple was then led from doubt to certainty, and from anguish of mind to the bliss of the Spirit. This, however, was not an easy attainment.

Sri Ramakrishna, perfect teacher that he was, never laid down identical disciplines for disciples of diverse temperaments. He did not insist that Narendra should follow strict rules about food, nor did he ask him to believe in the reality of the gods and goddesses of Hindu mythology. It was not necessary for Narendra's philosophic mind to pursue the disciplines of concrete worship. However, Naren practiced of discrimination, detachment, self-control, and regular meditation.

Sri Ramakrishna enjoyed Naren's vehement arguments with the other devotees regarding the dogmas and creeds of religion and was delighted to hear him tear to shreds their unquestioning beliefs. But when, as often happened, Naren teased the gentle Rakhal for showing reverence to the Divine Mother Kali, the Master would not tolerate these attempts to unsettle the brother disciple's faith in the forms of God.

As a member of the *Brahmo Samaj,* Narendra accepted its doctrine of monotheism and the Personal God. He also believed in the natural depravity of man. Such doctrines of non-dualistic Vedanta as the divinity of the soul and the oneness of existence, he regarded as blasphemy; the view that man is one with God appeared to him pure nonsense. When the master warned him against thus limiting God's infinitude and asked him to pray to God to reveal to him His true nature, Narendra smiled. One day he was making fun of Sri Ramakrishna's non-dualism before a friend and said, "What can be more absurd than to say that this jug is God, this cup is God, and that we too are God?" Both roared with laughter.

Just then the Master appeared. Coming to learn the cause of their fun, he gently touched Naren, who plunged into deep samadhi. The touch produced a magic effect, and Narendra entered a new realm of consciousness. He saw the whole universe permeated by the Divine Spirit and returned home in a daze. While eating his meal, he felt the presence of Brahman in everything—in the food, and in himself too. While walking in the street, he saw the carriages, the horses, the crowd, and himself, as if made of the same substance.

After a few days, the intensity of the vision lessened to some extent, but he still saw the world only as a dream. While strolling in a public park of Calcutta, he struck his head against the iron railing, several times, to see if they were real or a mere illusion of the mind. Thus, he got a glimpse of non-dualism, the fullest realization of which was to come only later, at the Cassipore garden.

Sri Ramakrishna used to be pleased, when his disciples put to test his statements or behaviour before accepting his teachings. He would say: "Test me as the money-changers test their coins. You must not believe me without testing me thoroughly." The disciples often heard him say that his nervous system had undergone a complete change as a result of his spiritual experiences, and that he could not bear the touch of any metal, such as gold or silver.

Naren, on the other hand, was often tested by the Master. One day, when he entered the Master's room, he was completely ignored. Not a word of greeting was uttered. A week later, he came back and met with the same indifference, and during the third and fourth visits saw no evidence of any thawing of the Master's frigid attitude.

At the end of a month Sri Ramakrishna said to Naren, "I have not exchanged a single word with you all this time, and still you come."

The disciple replied, "I come to Dakshineswar because I love you and want to see you. I do not come here to hear your words."

The Master was overjoyed. Embracing the disciple, he said, "I was only testing you. I wanted to see, if you would stay away on account of my outward indifference. Only a man of your inner strength could put up with such indifference on my part. Anyone else would have left me long ago."

On one occasion, Sri Ramakrishna proposed to transfer to Narendranath many of the spiritual powers that he had acquired as a result of his ascetic disciplines and visions of God. Naren had no doubt concerning the Master's possessing such powers. He asked, if they would help him to realize God. Sri Ramakrishna replied in the negative, but added that they might assist him in his future work as a spiritual teacher. "Let me realize God first," said Naren, "and then I shall perhaps know whether or not I want supernatural powers. If I accept them now, I may forget God, make selfish use of them, and thus come to grief." Sri Ramakrishna was highly pleased to see his chief disciple's single-minded devotion.

Several factors were at work to mould the personality of young Narendranath. Foremost of these were his inborn spiritual tendencies, which were beginning to show themselves under the influence of Sri Ramakrishna, but against which his rational mind put up a strenuous fight. Second was his habit of thinking highly and acting nobly, disciplines acquired from a mother steeped in the spiritual heritage of India. Third were his broadmindedness and regard for truth wherever found, and his sceptical attitude towards the religious beliefs and social conventions of the Hindu society of his time. These, he had learnt from his English-educated father, and he was strengthened in them through his own contact with Western culture.

With the introduction in India of English education during the middle of the nineteenth century, as we have seen, Western science, history, and philosophy were studied in the Indian colleges and universities. The educated Hindu youths, allured by the glamour, began to mould their thought according to this new light, and Narendra could not escape the influence.

He developed a great respect for the analytical scientific method and subjected many of the Master's spiritual visions to such scrutiny. The English poets stirred his feelings, especially Wordsworth and Shelley, and he took a course in Western medicine to understand the functioning of the nervous system, particularly the brain and spinal cord, in order to find out the secrets of Sri Ramakrishna's trances. But all this only deepened his inner turmoil.

John Stuart Mill's *Three Essays on Religion,* upset his boyish theism and the easy optimism imbibed from the *Brahmo Samaj*. The presence of evil in nature and man haunted him, and he could not reconcile it at all with the goodness of an omnipotent Creator. Hume's *Scepticism* and Herbert Spencer's *Doctrine of the Unknowable* filled his mind with a settled philosophical agnosticism. After the wearing out of his first emotional freshness and naivete, he was beset with a certain dryness and incapacity for the old prayers and devotions. He was filled with an ennui which he concealed, however, under his jovial nature. Music, at this difficult stage of his life, rendered him great help; for it moved him as nothing else and gave him a glimpse of unseen realities that often brought tears to his eyes.

Narendra, intensifying his meditation under the Master's guidance, began to lose consciousness of the body and to feel an inner peace, and this peace would linger even after the meditation was over. Frequently, he felt the separation of the body from the soul. Strange perceptions came to him in dreams, producing a sense of exaltation that persisted after he awoke. The guru was performing his task in an inscrutable manner. Narendra's friends observed only his outer struggle; but the real transformation was known to the teacher alone—or perhaps to the disciple too.

"Today," the Master continued, "is a Tuesday, an auspicious day for the Mother's worship. Go to Her shrine in the evening, prostrate yourself before the image, and pray to Her for any boon; it will be granted. Mother Kali is the embodiment of Love and Compassion. She is the Power of Brahman. She gives birth to the world by Her mere wish. She fulfils every sincere prayer of Her devotees."

At nine o'clock in the evening, Narendranath went to the Kali temple. Passing through the courtyard, he felt within himself a surge of emotion, and his heart leapt with joy in anticipation of the vision of the Divine Mother. Entering the temple, he cast his eyes upon the image and found the stone figure to be nothing else but the living Goddess, the Divine Mother Herself, ready to give him any boon he wanted—either a happy worldly life or the joy of spiritual freedom. He prayed for the boon of wisdom, discrimination, renunciation, and Her uninterrupted vision, but forgot to ask the Deity for money. He felt great peace within as he returned to the Master's room, and when asked, if he had prayed for money, was startled. He said that he had forgotten all about it. The Master told him to go to the temple again and pray to the Divine Mother to satisfy his immediate needs. Naren did as he was bidden, but again forgot his mission. The same thing happened a third time.

Then Naren suddenly realized that Sri Ramakrishna himself had made him forget to ask the Divine Mother for wordly things; perhaps he wanted Naren to lead a life of renunciation. So he now asked Sri Ramakrishna to do something for the family. The master told the disciple that it was not Naren's destiny to enjoy a worldly life, but assured him that the family would be able to eke out a simple existence.

The above incident left a deep impression upon Naren's mind; it enriched his spiritual life, for he gained a new understanding of the Godhead and its ways in the phenomenal universe. Naren's idea of God had hitherto been confined either to that of a vague Impersonal Reality or to that of an extra-cosmic Creator removed from the world.

He now realized that the Godhead is immanent in the creation, that after projecting the universe from within Itself, It has entered into all created entities as life and consciousness, whether manifest or latent. This same immanent Spirit, or the World Soul, when regarded as a person creating, preserving, and destroying the universe, is called the Personal God, and is worshipped by different religions, through such a relationship as that of father, mother, king, or beloved. These relationships, he came to understand, have their appropriate symbols, and Kali is one of them.

Embodying in Herself creation and destruction, love and terror, life and death, Kali is the symbol of the total universe. The eternal cycle of the manifestation and non-manifestation of the universe is the breathing-out and breathing-in of this Divine Mother. In one aspect, She is death, without which, there cannot be life. She is smeared with blood, since without blood the picture of the phenomenal universe is not complete. To the wicked, who have transgressed Her laws, She is the embodiment of terror, and to the virtuous, the benign Mother. To the daring devotee, who wants to see the transcendental Absolute, She reveals that form by withdrawing Her phenomenal aspect. Brahman is Her transcendental aspect. She is the Great Fact of the universe, the totality of created beings. She is the Ruler and the Controller.

All this had previously been beyond Narendra's comprehension. He had accepted the reality of the phenomenal world and yet denied the reality of Kali. He had been conscious of hunger and thirst, pain and pleasure, and the other characteristics of the world, and yet he had not accepted Kali, who controlled them all.

That was why, he had suffered. But on that auspicious Tuesday evening, the scales dropped from his eyes. He accepted Kali as the Divine Mother of the universe. He became Her devotee.

Many years later, he wrote to an American lady: "Kali worship is my special fad." But he did not preach Her in public, because he thought that all that modern man required was to be found in the Upanishads. Further, he realized that the Kali symbol would not be understood by universal humanity.

Narendra enjoyed the company of the Master for six years, during which time his spiritual life was moulded. Sri Ramakrishna was a wonderful teacher in every sense of the word. Without imposing his ideas upon anyone, he taught more by the silent influence of his inner life than by words or even by personal example. To live near him demanded of a disciple the purity of thought and the concentration of mind. He often appeared to his future monastic followers as their friend and playmate. Through fun and merriment, he always kept before them the shining ideal of God-realization. He would not allow any deviation from bodily and mental chastity, nor any compromise with truth and renunciation. Everything else he left to the will of the Divine Mother.

Narendra was his 'marked' disciple, chosen by the Lord for a special mission. Sri Ramakrishna kept a sharp eye on him, though he appeared to give the disciple every opportunity to release his pent-up physical and mental energy. Before him, Naren often romped about like a young lion cub in the presence of a firm but indulgent parent. His spiritual radiance often startled the Master, who saw that maya, the Great Enchantress, could not approach within 'ten feet' of that blazing fire.

Narendra always came to the Master in the hours of his spiritual difficulties. Once, he complained that he could not meditate in the morning on account of the shrill note of a whistle from a neighbouring mill, and was advised by the Master to concentrate on the very sound of the whistle. In a short time, he overcame the distraction. Next time, he found it difficult to forget the body at the time of meditation. Sri Ramakrishna sharply pressed the space between Naren's eyebrows and asked him to concentrate on that sensation.

Witnessing the religious ecstasy of several devotees, Narendra one day said to the Master that he too wanted to experience it. "My child," he was told, "when a huge elephant enters a small pond, a great commotion is set up, but when it plunges into the Ganga, the river shows very little agitation. These devotees are like small ponds; a little experience makes their feelings flow over the brim. But you are a huge river."

Another day, the thought of excessive spiritual fervour frightened Naren. The Master reassured him by saying, "God is like an ocean of sweetness; wouldn't you dive into it? Suppose there is a bowl filled with syrup, and you are a fly, hungry for the sweet liquid. How would you like to drink it?" Narendra said that he would sit on the edge of the bowl, otherwise, he might be drowned in the syrup and lose his life. "But," the Master said, "you must not forget that I am talking of the Ocean of Satchidananda, the Ocean of Immortality. Here, one need not be afraid of death. Only fools say that one should not have too much of divine ecstasy. Can anybody carry to excess the love of God? You must dive deep in the Ocean of God."

On one occasion Narendra and some of his brother disciples were vehemently arguing about God's nature

—whether He was personal or impersonal, whether Divine Incarnation was fact or myth, and so forth and so on. Narendra silenced his opponents by his sharp power of reasoning and felt jubilant at his triumph.

In his heart of hearts, Naren was a lover of God. Pointing to his eyes, Ramakrishna said that only a *bhakta* possessed such a tender look; the eyes of the *jnani* were generally dry. Many a time, in his later years, Narendra said, comparing his own spiritual attitude with that of the Master "He was a *jnani* within, but a *bhakta* without; but I am a *bhakta* within, and a *jnani* without." He meant that Ramakrishna's gigantic intellect was hidden under a thin layer of devotion, and Narendra's devotional nature was covered by a cloak of knowledge.

Sri Ramakrishna was worried about the distress of Naren's family and one day, asked a wealthy devotee, if he could help Naren financially. Naren's pride was wounded and he mildly scolded the Master. The latter said with tears in his eyes, "O my Naren! I can do anything for you, even beg from door to door." Narendra was deeply moved but said nothing. Many days after, he remarked, "The Master has made me his slave by his love for me."

This great love of Sri Ramakrishna enabled Naren to face calmly the hardships of life.

— *** —

WORTHY DISCIPLE OF A GREAT GURU

The poverty at home was not an altogether unmitigated evil. It drew out another side of Naren's character. He began to feel intensely for the needy and afflicted. Had he been nurtured in luxury, the Master used to say, he would perhaps have become a different person—a statesman, a lawyer, an orator, or a social reformer. But instead, he dedicated his life to the service of humanity.

Sri Ramakrishna had the prevision of Naren's future life of renunciation. Therefore, he was quite alarmed when he came to know of the various plans made by Naren's relatives for his marriage. Prostrating himself in the shrine of Kali, he prayed repeatedly, "O Mother! Do break up these plans. Do not let him sink in the quagmire of the world." He closely watched Naren and warned him whenever he discovered the trace of an impure thought in his mind.

Naren's keen mind understood the subtle implications of Sri Ramakrishna's teachings. One day the Master said that the three salient disciplines of Vaishnavism were love of God's name, service to the devotees, and compassion for all living beings. But he did not like the word compassion and said to the devotees, "How foolish to speak of compassion! Man is an insignificant worm crawling on the earth — and he to show compassion to others! This is absurd. It must not be compassion, but service to all. Recognise them as God's manifestations and serve them."

The other devotees heard the words of the Master but could hardly understand their significance. Taking his young friends aside, Naren said that Sri Ramakrishna's remarks had thrown wonderful light on the philosophy of non-dualism with its discipline of non-attachment, and on that of dualism with its discipline of love. The two were not really in conflict. A non-dualist did not have to make his heart dry as sand, nor did he have to run away from the world. As Brahman alone existed in all men, a non-dualist must love all and serve all. Love, in the true sense of the word, is not possible unless one sees God in every one. He also realised that an illumined person did not have to remain inactive; he could commune with Brahman through service to other embodied beings, who also are embodiments of Brahman.

"If it be the will of God," Naren concluded, "I shall one day proclaim this noble truth before the world at large. I shall make it the common property of all— the wise and the fool, the rich and the poor, the brahmin and the pariah."

It was Sri Ramakrishna, who re-educated Narendranath in the essentials of Hinduism. He, the fulfilment of the spiritual aspirations of the three hundred millions of Hindus for the past three thousand years, was the embodiment of the Hindu faith.

Narendra further learnt that religion is a vision which, at the end, transcends all barriers of caste and race and breaks down the limitations of time and space. He learnt from the Master that the Personal God and worship through symbols ultimately lead the devotee to the realization of complete oneness with the Deity. His master showed Naren by his own example, how a man in this very life could reach perfection, and the disciple found that the Master had realised the same God-consciousness by following the diverse disciplines of Hinduism, Christianity, and Islam.

One day, the Master in an ecstatic mood, said to the devotees, "There are many opinions and many ways. I have seen them all and do not like them any more. The devotees of different faiths quarrel among themselves. Let me tell you something. You are my own people. There are no strangers around. I clearly see that God is the whole and I am a part of Him. He is the Lord and I am His servant. And sometimes, I think, He is I and I am He.'

Narendra regarded Sri Ramakrishna as the embodiment of the spirit of religion and did not bother to know whether he was or not an Incarnation of God. It was enough for Naren, if he could see through the vista of Ramakrishna's spiritual experiences, all the aspects of the Godhead.

Narendra impress the other devotees of the Master, especially the youngsters. He was their idol. They were awed by his intellect and fascinated by his personality. He was graceful without being feminine. He had a strong jaw, suggesting his staunch will and fixed determination.

The most remarkable thing about him was his eyes, which Sri Ramakrishna compared to lotus petals. They were prominent but not protruding, and part of the time their gaze was indrawn, suggesting the habit of deep meditation; their colour varied according to the feeling of the moment. Sometimes, they would be luminous in profundity, and sometimes they sparkled in merriment. He walked sometimes with a slow gait and sometimes with rapidity, always a part of his mind absorbed in deep thought. And it was a delight to hear his resonant voice, either in conversation or in music.

But when Naren was serious, his face often frightened his friends. In a heated discussion, his eyes glowed. If immersed in his own thoughts, he created such an air of aloofness that no one dared to approach him. Subject to various moods, sometimes he showed utter impatience with his environment, and sometimes a tenderness that melted everybody's heart. His smile was bright and infectious. To some, he was a happy dreamer, to others, he lived in a real world rich with love and beauty, but to all, he unfailingly appeared a scion of an aristocratic home.

Naren was being literally consumed by a passion for God. The world appeared to him to be utterly distasteful. When the Master reminded him of his college studies, the disciple said, "I would feel relieved, if I could swallow a drug and forget all I have learnt." He spent night after night in meditation under the trees in the Panchavati at Dakshineswar, where Sri Ramakrishna, during the days of his spiritual discipline, had contemplated God. He felt the awakening of the Kundalini and had other spiritual visions.

One day at Cassipore, Narendra was meditating under a tree with Girish, another disciple. The place was infested with mosquitoes. Girish tried in vain to concentrate his mind. Casting his eyes on Naren, he saw him absorbed in meditation, though his body appeared to be covered by a blanket of the insects.

A few days later, Narendra's longing seemed to have reached the breaking-point. He spent an entire night walking around the garden house at Cassipore and repeating Rama's name in a heart-rending manner. In the early hours of the morning, Sri Ramakrishna heard his voice, called him to his side, and said affectionately, "Listen, my child, why are you acting that way? What will you achieve by such impatience?" He stopped for a minute and then continued, "See, Naren. What you have been doing now, I did for twelve long years. A storm raged in my head during that period. What will you realize in one night?"

But the master was pleased with Naren's spiritual struggle and made no secret of his wish to make him his spiritual heir. He wanted Naren to look after the young disciples. "I leave them in your care," he said to him, "love them intensely and see that they practise spiritual disciplines even after my death, and that they do not return home." He asked the young disciples to regard Naren as their leader. It was an easy task for them. Then, one day, Sri Ramakrishna initiated several of the young disciples into the monastic life, and thus himself laid the foundation of the future Ramakrishna Order of Monks.

Attendance on the Master during his sickness revealed to Narendra the true import of Sri Ramakrishna's spiritual experiences. He was amazed to find that the Master could dissociate himself from all consciousness of the body by a mere wish, at which time he was not aware of the least pain due to his ailment. He constantly enjoyed an inner bliss, in spite of the suffering of the body, and he could transmit that bliss to the disciples by a mere touch or look. To Narendra, Sri Ramakrishna was the vivid demonstration of the reality of the Spirit and the unsubstantiality of matter.

One day, the Master was told by a scholar that he could instantly cure himself of his illness by concentrating his mind on his throat. This, Sri Ramakrishna refused to do, since he could never withdraw his mind from God. But at Naren's repeated request, the Master agreed to speak to the Divine Mother about his illness. A little later he said to the disciple in a sad voice: "Yes, I told Her that I could not swallow any food on account of the sore in my throat, and asked Her to do something about it. But the Mother said, pointing to you all, 'Why, are you not eating enough through all these mouths?' I felt so humiliated that I could not utter another word." Narendra realized how Sri Ramakrishna applied in life the Vedantic idea of the oneness of existence and also came to know that only through such realization could one rise above the pain and suffering of the individual life.

To live with Sri Ramakrishna during his illness was in itself a spiritual experience. It was wonderful to witness how he bore with his pain. In one mood, he would see that the Divine Mother alone was the dispenser of pleasure and pain and that his own will was one with the Mother's will, and in another mood, he would clearly behold, the utter absence of diversity, God alone becoming men, animals, gardens, houses, roads, 'the executioner, the victim, and the slaughter-post,' to use the Master's own words.

Narendra saw in the Master, the living explanation of the scriptures regarding the divine nature of the soul and the illusoriness of the body. Further, he came to know that Sri Ramakrishna had attained to that state by the total renunciation of 'woman' and 'gold,' which, indeed, was the gist of his teaching. Another idea was creeping into Naren's mind. He began to see how the transcendental Reality, the Godhead, could embody Itself as the

Personal God, and the Absolute become a Divine Incarnation. He was having a glimpse of the greatest of all divine mysteries: the incarnation of the Father as the Son for the redemption of the world. He began to believe that God becomes man so that man may become God. Sri Ramakrishna thus appeared to him in a new light.

Under the intellectual leadership of Narendranath, the Cassipore garden house became a miniature university. During the few moments' leisure snatched from nursing and meditation, Narendra would discuss with his brother disciples religions and philosophies, both Eastern and Western. Along with the teachings of Sankara, Krishna, and Chaitanya, those of Buddha and Christ were searchingly examined.

Narendra had a special affection for Buddha, and one day suddenly felt a strong desire to visit Bodh-Gaya, where the great Prophet had attained enlightenment. With Kali and Tarak, two of the brother disciples, he left, unknown to the others, for that sacred place and meditated for long hours under the sacred Bo-tree. Once while thus absorbed, he was overwhelmed with emotion , embraced Tarak. Explaining the incident, he said afterwards that during the meditation, he keenly felt the presence of Buddha and saw vividly how the history of India had been changed by his noble teachings.

Back in Cassipore, Narendra described enthusiastically to the Master and the brother disciples of Buddha's life, experiences, and teachings. Sri Ramakrishna in turn related some of his own experiences. Narendra had to admit that the Master, after the attainment of the highest spiritual realization, had of his own will kept his mind on the phenomenal plane.

He further understood that a coin, however valuable, which belonged to an older period of history, could not be used as currency at a later date. God assumes different forms in different ages to serve the special needs of the time.

Narendra practised spiritual disciplines with unabating intensity. Sometimes, he felt an awakening of a spiritual power that he could transmit to others. One night in March 1886, he asked his brother disciple Kali to touch his right knee, and then entered into deep meditation. Kali's hand began to tremble; he felt a kind of electric shock. Afterwards, Narendra was rebuked by the Master for frittering away spiritual powers before accumulating them in sufficient measure. He was further told that he had injured Kali's spiritual growth, which had been following the path of dualistic devotion, by forcing upon the latter some of his own non-dualistic ideas. The Master added, however, that the damage was not serious.

Narendra had enough of visions and manifestations of spiritual powers, and he now wearied of them. His mind longed for the highest experience of non-dualistic

Vedanta, the nirvikalpa samadhi, in which the names and forms of the phenomenal world disappear and the aspirant realizes total non-difference between the individual soul, the universe, and Brahman, or the Absolute. He told Sri Ramakrishna about it, but the master remained silent. And yet one evening the experience came to him quite unexpectedly.

He was absorbed in his usual meditation when he suddenly felt, as if a lamp were burning at the back of his head. The light glowed more and more intensely and finally burst.

Narendra was overwhelmed by that light and fell unconscious. After some time, as he began to regain his normal mood, he could feel only his head and not the rest of his body. In an agitated voice he said to Gopal, a brother disciple who was meditating in the same room, "Where is my body?"

Gopal answered: "Why, Naren, it is there. Don't you feel it?"

Gopal was afraid that Narendra was dying, and ran to Sri Ramakrishna's room. He found the Master in a calm but serious mood, evidently aware of what had happened in the room downstairs. After listening to Gopal, the Master said, "Let him stay in that state for a while; he has teased me long enough for it."

For some time, Narendra remained unconscious. When he regained his normal state of mind, he was bathed in an ineffable peace. As he entered Sri Ramakrishna's room, the latter said: "Now the Mother has shown you everything. But this realization, like the jewel locked in a box, will be hidden away from you and kept in my custody. I will keep the key with me. Only after you have fulfilled your mission on this earth, will the box be unlocked, and you will know everything as you have known now."

The experience of this kind of samadhi usually has a most devastating effect upon the body; Incarnations and special messengers of God alone can survive its impact. By way of advice, Sri Ramakrishna asked Naren to use great discrimination about his food and companions, only accepting the purest.

Later, the master said to the other disciples: "Narendra will give up his body of his own will. When he realizes his true nature, he will refuse to stay on this earth. Very soon, he will shake the world by his intellectual and spiritual powers. I have prayed to the Divine Mother to keep away from him the Knowledge of the Absolute and cover his eyes with a veil of maya. There is much work to be done by him. But the veil, I see, is so thin that it may be rent at any time."

Sri Ramakrishna, the Avatar of the modern age, was too gentle and tender to labour himself, for humanity's welfare. He needed some sturdy souls to carry on his work.

Narendra was foremost among those around him; therefore, Sri Ramakrishna did not want him to remain immersed in nirvikalpa samadhi before his task in this world was finished.

The disciples sadly watched the gradual wasting away of Sri Ramakrishna's physical frame. His body became a mere skeleton covered with skin; the suffering was intense. But he devoted his remaining energies to the training of the disciples, especially Narendra. He had been relieved of his worries about Narendra; for the disciple now admitted the divinity of Kali, whose will controls all things in the universe. Naren said later on: "From the time he gave me over to the Divine Mother, he retained the vigour of his body only for six months. The rest of the time—and that was two long years—he suffered."

One day the Master, unable to speak even in a whisper, wrote on a piece of paper: "Narendra will teach others." The disciple demurred. Sri Ramakrishna replied: "But you must. Your very bones will do it." He further said that all the supernatural powers he had acquired would work through his beloved disciple.

A short while before the curtain finally fell on Sri Ramakrishna's earthly life, the Master one day called Naren to his bedside. Gazing intently upon him, he passed into deep meditation. Naren felt that a subtle force, resembling an electric current, was entering his body. He gradually lost outer consciousness. After some time, he regained knowledge of the physical world and found the Master weeping. Sri Ramakrishna said to him: "O Naren, today I have given you everything I possess—now I am no more than a fakir, a penniless beggar. By the powers I have transmitted to you, you will accomplish great things in the world, and not until then will you return to the source, whence you have come".

Narendra from that day became the channel of Sri Ramakrishna's powers and the spokesman of his message.

Two days before the dissolution of the Master's body, Narendra was standing by the latter's bedside, when a strange thought flashed into his mind: "Was the Master truly an Incarnation of God?" He said to himself that he would accept Sri Ramakrishna's divinity if the Master, on the threshold of death, declared himself to be an Incarnation. He stood looking intently at the Master's face. Slowly, Sri Ramakrishna's lips parted and he said in a clear voice: "O my Naren, are you still not convinced? He, who in the past was born as Rama and Krishna is now living in this very body as Ramakrishna—but not from the standpoint of your Vedanta." Thus Sri Ramakrishna, in answer to Narendra's mental query, put himself in the category of Rama and Krishna, who are recognised by orthodox Hindus as two of the Avatars, or Incarnations of God.

A few words may be said here about the meaning of the Incarnation in the Hindu religious tradition. One of the main doctrines of Vedanta is the divinity of the soul: every soul, in reality, is Brahman. Thus, it may be presumed that there is no difference between an Incarnation and an ordinary man. To be sure, from the standpoint of the Absolute, or Brahman, no such difference exists.

But from the relative standpoint, where multiplicity is perceived, a difference must be admitted. Embodied human beings reflect godliness in varying measure. In an Incarnation, this godliness is fully manifest. Therefore, an Incarnation is unlike an ordinary mortal or even an illumined saint. There is no difference between a clay lion and a clay mouse, from the standpoint of the clay. Both become the same substance when dissolved into clay.

But the difference between the lion and the mouse, from the standpoint of form, is clearly seen. Likewise, as Brahman, an ordinary man is identical with an Incarnation. Both become the same Brahman when they attain final illumination.

THE PHILOSOPHY OF SWAMI

Vivekananda was a renowned thinker in his own right. One of his most important contributions was to demonstrate, how Advaitin thinking is not merely philosophically far-reaching, but how it also has social, even political, consequences. One important lesson he claimed to receive from Ramakrishna was that "*Jiva is Shiva*" (each individual is divinity itself). This became his Mantra, and he coined the concept of *daridra narayana seva* - the service of God in and through (poor) human beings. If, there truly is the unity of Brahman underlying all phenomena, then on what basis do we regard ourselves as better or worse, or even as better-off or worse-off, than others? This was the question he posed to himself. Ultimately, he concluded that these distinctions fade into nothingness in the light of the oneness that the devotee experiences in Moksha. What arises then is compassion for those "individuals" who remain unaware of this oneness and a determination to help them.

Vivekananda did not advocate the emerging area of parapsychology and astrology (one instance can be found in his speech *Man the Maker of his Destiny, Complete-Works, Volume 8, Notes of Class Talks and Lectures*) saying that this form of curiosity does not help in spiritual progress but actually hinders it.

Swami Vivekananda belonged to that branch of Vedanta that held that no-one can be truly free until all of us are. Even the desire for personal salvation has to be given up, and only tireless work for the salvation of others is the true mark of the enlightened person.

Vivekananda advised to be holy, unselfish and have shraddha (faith). He encouraged the practise of Brahmacharya (Celibacy). In one of the conversations with his childhood friend Sri Priya Nath Sinha, he attributes his physical and mental strengths, as also eloquence to the practice of brahmacharya.

However, Vivekananda also pleaded for a strict separation between religion and government ("church and state"). Although social customs had been formed in the past with religious sanction, it was not now the business of religion to interfere with matters such as marriage, inheritance and so on. The ideal society would be a mixture of Brahmin knowledge, Kshatriya culture, Vaisya efficiency and the egalitarian Shudra ethos. Domination by any one led to different sorts of lopsided societies. Vivekananda did not feel that religion, nor, any force for that matter, should be used forcefully to bring about an ideal society, since this was something that would evolve naturally by individualistic change, when the conditions were right.

The turban that Vivekananda used to wear is generally believed to be suggested by Maharaja of Khetri. But some people claim that Vivekananda visited the Swamithope Pathi during his visit to Kanyakumari in December, 1892 and believe that he was impressed by the principles behind rituals of this monistic faith, such as wearing a head gear during worship in temple, worshipping in front of mirror etc., and started wearing a turban from then on. Some also suggest that Vivekananda received some spiritual instructions from the disciples of Ayya Vaikundar. There is no mention of this in Vivekananda's biographies or works. It is also said that while he was a child, he was impresssed by the turban of the horse cab driver, who used to ferry his father on his daily work. Subsequently, when he renounced the world and took to sanyasa, he started using one himself.

Swami Vivekananda inspired India's freedom struggle movement. His writings inspired a whole generation of freedom fighters in Bengal in particular and India at large. Some of the most prominent amongst them were Subhas Chandra Bose, Aurobindo and countless others.

He died in 1902, at the age of 39. After his death, he left behind an enormous wealth of inspiration and instruction on the yogas (karma, jnana, bhakti), as well as on various other aspects of the spiritual process.

— *** —

SAYINGS OF SWAMI VIVEKANANDA

➢ My ideal, indeed, can be put into a few words, and that is to preach unto mankind their divinity, and how to make it manifest in every movement of life.

➢ Religion is the manifestation of the divinity already in man.

➢ Religion is the idea which is raising the brute unto man, and man unto God.

➢ The secret of religion lies not in theories but in practice. To be good and do good–that is the whole of religion.

➢ Man is higher than all animals, than all angels; none is greater than man.

➢ One may gain political and social independence, but if one is a slave to his passions and desires, one cannot feel the pure joy of real freedom.

➢ Look at the wall. Did the wall ever tell a lie? It is always the wall. Man tells a lie and becomes a god, too.

➢ After so much austerity, I have understood this as the real truth–God is present in every jiva; there is no other God besides that. 'Who serves jiva, serves God indeed.'

➤ Cut out the word help from your mind. You cannot help; it is blasphemy! You worship. When you give a morsel of food to a dog, you worship the dog as God. He is all, and is in all.

➤ Unselfishness is God. One may live on a throne, in a palace, and be perfectly unselfish; and then he is in God. Another may live in a hut and wear rags, and have nothing in the world; yet if he is selfish, he is intensely merged in the world.

➤ All nations have attained greatness by paying proper respect to women. That country and that nation which do not respect women have never become great, nor will ever be in future.

➤ With five hundred men, ... the conquest of India might take fifty years: with as many women, not more than a few weeks.

➤ Religion and religion alone is the life of India, and when that goes, India will die, in spite of politics, in spite of social reforms, in spite of Kubera's wealth poured upon the head of every one of her children.

➤ Before flooding India with socialistic or political ideas, first deluge the land with spiritual ideas.

➤ We want to lead mankind to the place where there is neither the Vedas, nor the Bible, nor the Koran; yet this has to be done by harmonizing the Vedas, the Bible, and the Koran.

➢   Mankind ought to be taught that religions are but the varied expressions of THE RELIGION, which is Oneness, so that each may choose the path that suits him best.

➢   Who will give the world light? Sacrifice in the past has been the Law, it will be, alas, for ages to come. The earth's bravest and best will have to sacrifice themselves for the good of many, for the welfare of all.

➢   Truth, purity, and unselfishness–whenever these are present, there is no power below or above the sun to crush the possessor thereof. Equipped with these, one individual is able to face the whole universe in opposition.

➢   Everything can be sacrificed for truth, but truth cannot be sacrificed for anything.

➢   The highest ideal is eternal and entire self-abnegation, where there is no 'I', but is 'Thou'.

➢   All expansion is life, all contraction is death.

➢   All love is expansion, all selfishness is contraction. Love is, therefore, the only law of life. He who loves lives, he who is selfish is dying. Therefore, love for love's sake, because it is law of life, just as you breathe to live.

➢   The national ideals of India are Renunciation and Service. Intensify her in those channels, and the rest will take care of itself.

➤   Good motives, sincerity, and infinite love can conquer the world. One single soul possessed of these virtues can destroy the dark designs of millions of hypocrites and brutes.

➤   Take up one idea. Make that one idea your life—think of it, dream of it, live on idea. Let the brain, muscles, nerves, every part of your body, be full of that idea, and just leave every other idea alone. This is the way to success.

➤   "Remember!" he said once to a disciple, "Remember! the message of India is always "Not the soul for nature, but nature for the soul !"

➤   "He (Shri Ramakrishna) was contented simply to live that great life and to leave it to others to find the explanation!"

➤   "Ramakrishna Paramhamsa was the only man who ever had the courage to say that we must speak to all men in their own language!"

➤   "The older I grow, the more everything seems to me to lie in manliness. This is my new gospel."

➤   "You may always say that the image is God. The error you have to avoid is to think God is the image."

➤   "Love is always a manifestation of bliss. The least shadow of pain falling upon it is always a sign of physicality and selfishness."

➤   Strength is in goodness, in purity.

➢ "What is this idea of Bhakti without renunciation? It is most pernicious."

➢ "We worship neither pain nor pleasure. We seek through either to come at that which transcends them both."

➢ "The river is pure that flows, the monk is pure that goes!"

➢ "The Sannyasin who thinks of gold, to desire it, commits suicide."

➢ "If a bad time comes, what of that? The pendulum must swing back to the other side. But that is no better. The thing to do is to stop it."

➢ Man is born to conquer nature and not to follow it. When you think you are a body, you are apart from the universe; when you think you are a soul, you are a spark from the great Eternal Fire; when you think you are the Atman (Self), you are All.

➢ The will is not free–it is a phenomenon bound by cause and effect–but there is something behind the will which is free.

➢ The universe is–objectified God.

➢ You cannot believe in God until you believe in yourself.

➢ The root of evil is in the illusion that we are bodies. This, if any, is the original sin.